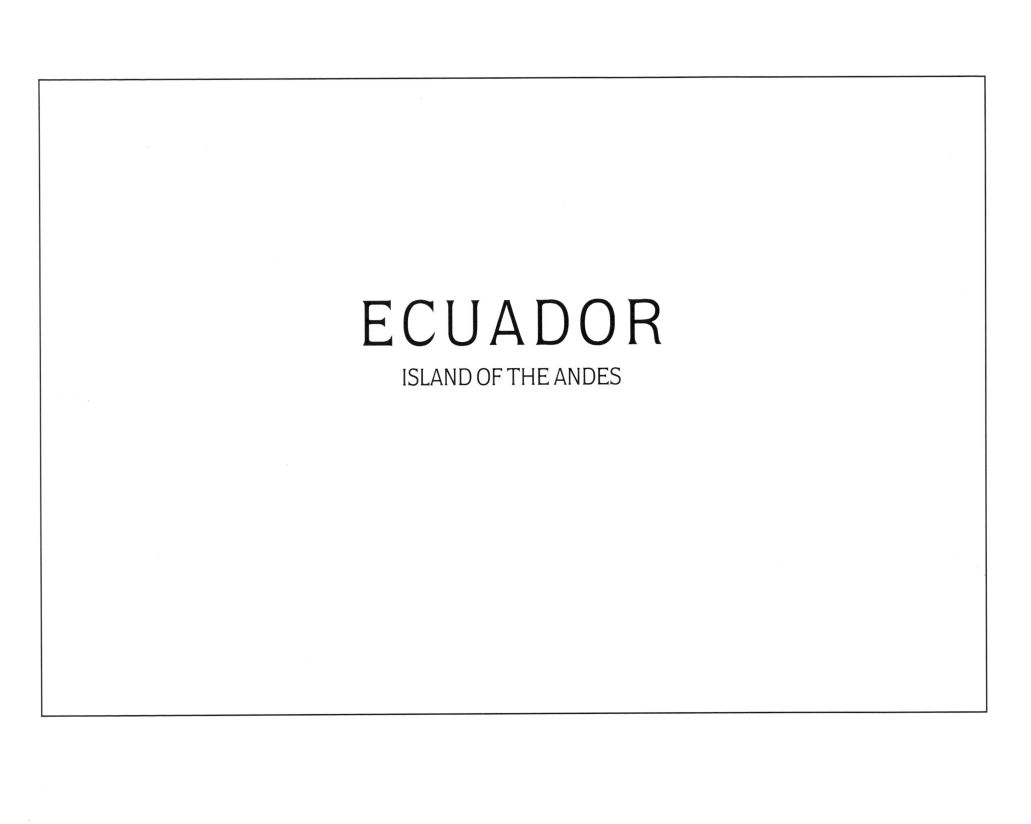

ECUADOR

ISLAND OF THE ANDES

KKOCHO A PACHAMAMA

Suttiquita aisarispa
qaillaicamuni, Pachamama
Yawar qonqorlla suchuspa
chaijatamuni, Pachamama
Panti tticata masttaspa
k'umuicamuni, Pachamama
Qori qaqa k'uichi ppacha
qoillor ttiquita, Pachamama
Imantintin munainiyoi
may tucuy ricuj, Pachaqaman
Janajpacha k'anchajqocha
kollke aquilla, Pachaqaman
Inti kkoni causaitapas
aipullawaicu, Pachaqaman
Unu para qarpatapas
chchajchumuwaicu, Pachaqaman
Ama yareqai watapas
chayamuchunchu, Pachaqaman
Wajcha wawaiquicunata
ricullawaicu, Pachaqaman.

PRAYER TO MOTHER EARTH

Calling on thy name,
I approach thee, Mother Earth;
With bleeding knees,
I come to thee, Mother Earth;
Scattering *panti* flowers,
I bow before thee, Mother Earth;
Golden gem, rainbow robe,
starry flower, Mother Earth.
All-powerful Lord
who seeth all, Pachaqaman;
Celestial lake,
silver vase, Pachaqaman;
Grant us the sun's heat,
source of life, Pachaqaman;
And with thy rain
sprinkle us, Pachaqaman;
Preserve us
from devouring hunger, Pachaqaman;
The orphan children,
forget them not, Pachaqaman.

From the album *Sartañani* by the group 'Bolivia Manta' (Auvidis)

ECUADOR
ISLAND OF THE ANDES

Photographs by Kevin Kling

Text by Kevin Kling and Nadia Christensen

with 100 color photographs and a map

Thames and Hudson

For my parents

ACKNOWLEDGMENTS

At the outset, every adventure is like a play in which one does not know the characters. They make their appearance as the journey unfolds. I am grateful to them all for the riches that they have brought me. Above all, Marcela Garcia, who lavished friendship and hospitality on me and allowed me to discover the most secret places of her country. My gratitude also to Martha and Michel Rowland, Patricio Garcia, Eduardo Vega, the Chiriboga family of Zuleta, Mariano Proaño and Pablo Burbano of Metropolitan Tours, Daniel Kupermann, Señor Leiva, Pedro Abril, Claire Lambea and the Auvidis record company. Also to Carlos and Julio Arguedas and their group 'Bolivia Manta', as well as to the group 'Ñanda Mañachi', for the inspiration that they gave me through their Andean music. Finally, I would like to thank Ximena Parga-Yávar, Evelyne Second, Anne Collin Delavaud, Nathalie Nekhoul, the Laboratoire Picto, Paris, and *GEO* magazine for their help, and Paul Tapponnier for his constant support.

First published in the USA in 1988 by Thames and Hudson Inc., 500 Fifth Avenue, New York, New York 10110

Originally published in France as *Equateur, Ile des Indes* in 1987 by Editions du Chêne, Paris

Printed and bound in Switzerland

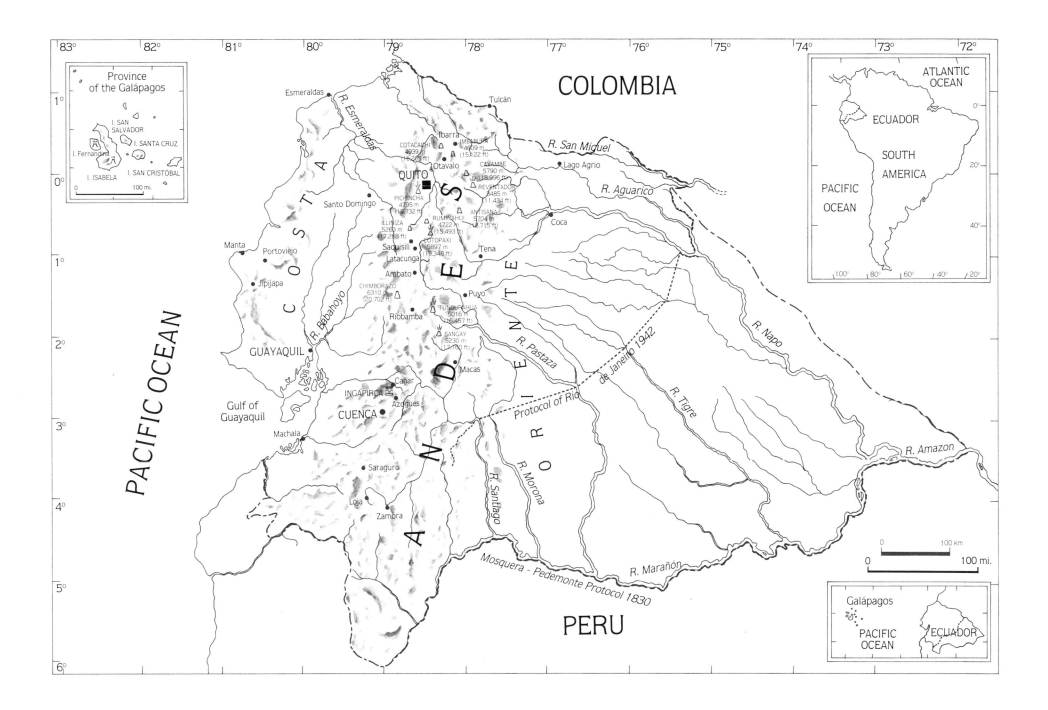

COLOMBIA

PERU

PACIFIC OCEAN

Province
of the Galápagos

I. SAN
SALVADOR
I. SANTA CRUZ
I. Fernandina
I. ISABELA   I. SAN CRISTÓBAL

0   100 mi.

ATLANTIC
OCEAN

ECUADOR

SOUTH
AMERICA

PACIFIC
OCEAN

Galápagos

PACIFIC
OCEAN   ECUADOR

Esmeraldas
Tulcán
R. San Miguel
Ibarra
COTACACHI   IMBABURA
4939 m   4609 m
(16,205 ft)   (15,122 ft)
Otavalo   CAYAMBE   Lago Agrio
5790 m
(18,996 ft)
QUITO
REVENTADOR
5485 m
(11,434 ft)
PICHINCHA
4795 m   ANTISANA
(15,732 ft)   5704 m
(12,715 ft)   Coca
Santo Domingo
ILLINIZA   RUMINAHUI
5263 m   4722 m
(17,268 ft)   (15,493 ft)
Manta   COTOPAXI
5897 m
Portoviejo   (19,348 ft)   Tena
Saquisilí
Latacunga
Jipijapa   Ambato
CHIMBORAZO
6310 m   Puyo
(20,702 ft)
Riobamba   TUNGURAHUA
5016 m
(16,457 ft)
SANGAY
5230 m
(17,160 ft)
GUAYAQUIL   Macas
Cañar
INGAPIRCA
Azogues
Gulf of   CUENCA
Guayaquil
Machala
Saraguro
Loja
Zamora

R. Esmeraldas
R. Aguarico
R. Napo
R. Babahoyo
R. Pastaza
R. Tigre
R. Amazon
R. Santiago
R. Morona
R. Marañón

de Janeiro 1942
Protocol of Rio
Mosquera - Pedemonte Protocol 1830

COSTA
ANDES
ORIENTE

0   100 km

0   100 mi.

1   Pujili, Sunday Mass.
2   Before a storm, Imbabura Province.
3   Ripe wheat, Imbabura Province.
4   Break in the clouds near Imbabura.
5   Fertile hills west of Cuicocha Lake.
6   Swaying eucalyptus trees, northern Sierra.
7   Threshold of a *finca*, region of Otavalo.
8   Zuleta girl with a white rooster.
9   Volcanic mesa, north of Otavalo.
10 Evening sun near San Pablo.
11 Cotopaxi, one of the world's highest active volcanoes.
12 Chota Valley, northern highlands.
13 Cayambe, pinnacle of the equator.
14 Sheep pen, Imbabura Province.
15 Complicity, San Juan fiesta, Zuleta.
16 The San Juan fiesta in Zuleta is a time to wear one's best clothes and forget about work.
17 The *loa* procession circles the hacienda, San Juan day, Zuleta.
18 Even babies taste *chicha* during the San Juan fiesta.
19 Zuleta woman.
20 In Otavalo, the colour and style of folding of headdresses (*fachalinas*) indicate local origin and marital status.
21 Sierra flowers.
22 High-altitude pastures, northern Sierra.
23 Riding horse, Zuleta.
24 Reminiscing in the shade, San Juan fiesta.
25 Maize and barley thrive up to 4,000 m (13,000 ft) or the equator.
26 Fields of *quinoa*, grown only in the Andes, make orange patches on the highest slopes.
27 Road to Cayambe.
28 Harvest time, Bolívar Province.
29 It is the blanket of pink and white volcanic ash that makes Andean slopes fertile, Azuay Province.
30 Otavalo girl.
31 Indian women of the northern Sierra like to wear several strands of glass-blown gold beads.
32 A home at the foot of Cayambe.
33 Valley and ridges, Loja Province.
34 *Maguey* plants delineate family plots of the Salasaca Indians.
35 Church in front of Tungurahua.
36 Cuenca market.
37 Bargaining for cloth, Riobamba.
38 Puruhua Indian and baby.
39 Saraguro men often wear white panama hats, but always keep their hair in a single long braid.
40 *Cholo* girl in a pink shawl, Pujili market.
41 Squealing piglets, Saquisili market.
42 Puruhua girl, Riobamba.
43 Sunday market at Pujili.
44 Saquisili Thursday market.
45 First purchase, Saquisili.
46 Heavy basket, Riobamba.
47 Ice falls on the equator, Cotopaxi.
48 Coastal marshland and water hyacinths, Gulf of Guayaquil.
49 Black volcanic rock and white coral sand, South Plaza Island, Galápagos.
50 Point Espinosa, Fernandina Island, Galápagos.
51 Crater Lake, Colombian border.
52 *Frailejones* grow above 4,000 m (13,000 ft) on volcanic *paramos*, Carchi Province.
53 *Frailejones* conquer the *paramo* slopes.
54 The abundant yield of hard work in the central highlands, near Guaranda.
55 Ingapirca, 'Wall of the Incas'.
56 Sowing seeds, Cañar Province.
57 A Cañari child takes a mid-afternoon break from work in the fields.
58 Red woollen ponchos, near Biblián.
59 Spinning and tilling at 4,200 m (13,800 ft), Cañar Province.
60 Cañari children and their dog keep one another warm.
61 Cañari cowboy.
62 A Salasaca *danzante* wears traditional wig and *banda* (cape), Corpus Christi fiesta.
63 *Pingullo* flute player, Corpus Christi fiesta, Salasaca.
64 *Maestros* and *danzantes* entertain at each Salasaca household during a Corpus Christi fiesta day.
65-66 Salasaca women celebrate Octavario Octava.
67 Salasaca women fasten their woven shawls with ornate silver pins called *topos*.
68 Salasaca fiestas mix traditional Indian and Catholic beliefs, costumes and symbols.
69 Salasaca men wear black ponchos, said to be a sign of mourning for the last Inca.
70 Sharing *chicha*, Corpus Christi fiesta.
71 Volcanic cliff, Loja Province.
72 Red and pink ash-flow tuffs, Loja Province.
73 Traditionally, Saraguros wear thick, wide-brimmed felt hats and carry double shoulder bags called *alforjas*.

74 Bakery, Saraguro.
75 Shopping with mother and father, Saraguro.
76 Sunday picnic, Saraguro.
77 Watching the cowherd, Saraguro highlands.
78 Alternating rows of *quinoa*, potatoes and barley in front of cloud-shrouded Altar.
79 Sheep graze in stubble-fields, Chimborazo Province.
80 Striped slopes beneath Chimborazo.
81 Freshly ploughed furrows, Chimborazo highlands.
82 Patchwork of crops at 4,200 m (13,800 ft).
83 Cultivated fields stretch up steep mountainsides as high as altitude permits.

84 *Chozas* near Chimborazo.
85 Puruhua shepherd girl.
86 Introduced by the Spanish, donkeys are more common than llamas in Ecuador.
87 Lone Puruhua boy with his sheep.
88 Resting on the hillside.
89 Shepherdess and baby, edge of Chimborazo *paramo*.
90 Morning snow powders the summit of Illiniza.
91 Instead of a harrow, leafy branches are used as a tool to cover seeds with earth.
92 Puruhuas must endure the hardships of farming above 4,000 m (13,000 ft).

93 Dusk at the foot of Chimborazo.
94 Running in the cold wind and dust, a young Puruhua shepherdess brandishes a stick to hasten the flock home before nightfall.
95 'Father' Chimborazo, the highest peak in Ecuador.
96 Like most highland pastoral dwellers, Puruhuas spin wool.
97 Tending the flocks is also the work of children.
98 Puruhua schoolgirl.
99 Mountain path, Chimborazo Province.
100 In the Andes, a child's work is not play — it carries true responsibility.

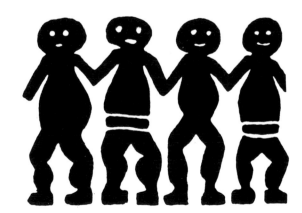

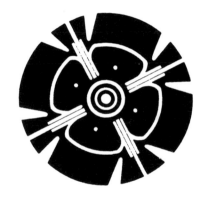

ECUADOR
ON THE
EQUATOR

1

The crescent moon lies horizontally above Cayambe. High over that peak, here at the equator, the new moon appears to rest on its back instead of standing upright as it does at more northerly latitudes.

To Indians of the Ecuadorian Andes it seems only natural that the moon grows full from a horizontal position. This is what they, and their ancestors, have witnessed. This is an age-old celestial pattern that they see as part of *Pachamama*, the Mother Earth whom they revere and love.

They find it natural, too, that in their world days and nights are constant and of equal length. Twelve hours of light, twelve hours of darkness, three hundred and sixty-five days of the year. At noon the sun blazes directly overhead, creating no shadow. Evening is a luminous half hour before the black curtain of night drops suddenly.

When darkness falls, the temperature falls abruptly, too — often by as much as 15°C (27°F). And the mountain winds, which are an Indian's constant companion, tug even harder at his woollen poncho.

Nowhere else on the equator are there such high mountains. Here climate is determined by altitude, rather than by latitude as on the rest of the globe. With every few hundred feet an Indian climbs he feels the temperature change, but because he is at the equator he does not encounter snow until about 5,000 m (16,500 ft). In his world, even mountains as high as Mont Blanc are never capped with ice.

The jagged peaks that tower above him are the backbone of Ecuador. Ridging the land from north to south, the mountains divide into two separate ranges dominated by more than thirty volcanoes. Lords of the Andes, these lone, brooding giants are the source of all mystery for the Indians who live in their shadow.

East of the Andes are the steaming jungles of the upper Amazon; to the west, the Pacific Ocean. An overwhelming variety of the earth's most imposing forms of nature — ocean, jungle, mountains, volcanoes — is crammed into this small country (283,520 km^2; 109,467 sq. mi.) about the size of Nevada or half that of France.

Most Indians make their homes in only one part of it: the Sierra, as the mountain region is called. Here, in the highland valleys, and in the cold, dry *paramo* stretching up the slopes at 3,000–4,000 m (10,000–13,000 ft) live nearly half of Ecuador's eight million people. About seven out of ten are Indians: Otavalos, Salasacas, Saraguros, Cañari, Puruhuas.

The roots of these Indians reach deep into Andean soil. Long before the Spanish conquest, before even the Incas came, some of their ancestors eked a living from these same mountainsides. The Indians are the link between Ecuador's past and present. They, too, are its backbone — strong and enduring, like the Andes themselves.

3

Fiestas are more than just celebrations for an Indian of the Sierra. They provide the only interruption in an endless rhythm of working from dawn to dusk. They divide the year, creating a pattern as regular as winter and summer seasons in other latitudes.

Throughout the northern Sierra, the year's greatest fiesta comes at the end of June. Originally, it was a pagan feast of the summer solstice. When the Spanish came, their priests wisely did not try to suppress such festivals; rather, they converted the celebrations to Catholicism by adding a Mass and a saint's day. The summer solstice coincides with the day of St John. So now it is in the name of San Juan that the Indians joke and drink and sing and fight and dance.

For more than a week they celebrate. Day and night; night and day. The highland valleys echo with shouts of *'Churay! Churay!'* Far over the Andes floats the plaintive, haunting music of Indian flutes, panpipes and guitars. From time to time come the discordant tones of brass bands made up of *cholos*, mestizos of Indian and Spanish blood, who are as numerous as Indians in Ecuador (each forms about forty per cent of the population).

Again and again, the same monotonous, four-measure tune is played – the San Juan fiesta tune. Swaying to the rhythm, their pounding feet raising clouds of summer dust, the Indians dance without resting. *'Llapi, llapi!* (Stamp, stamp!) *Sinche, sinche!* (Hard, hard!) *Tigrashpa, tigrashpa!* (Turn, turn!) *Jalajajaja!'* They dance uphill at 4,000 m (13,000 ft) breathing the thin mountain air. They show tremendous endurance.

Among the Zuleta Indians, the first day of the San Juan fiesta is a chance for a few to masquerade, to clown. A guitarist has bright streamers on his hat that hide his face; a flute player wears fur chaps. Following closely behind them is the 'little devil'. Others choose costumes imitating whites, who are a small minority in Ecuador (about ten per cent of the population). Disguised as soldiers, as hacienda owners or managers, they join the throngs of other Indians in a whirl of vibrant colour. Singing and shouting, they swarm into the yard of the white hacienda owner, on whose vast holding most of them work.

Today is a day to forget their labour. Today is a day to circle the owner's house, playing the San Juan tune. It is a day to give him twelve chickens that are strung on a horse which is festively decorated with mirrors and blankets. On another horse, just as gaily ornamented, rides the *loa* or praise-maker, a boy of about ten years old. His eyes are bright with nervous excitement as he recites, with dramatic voice and gestures, traditional verses from the Gospel of St John.

During each day of the festivities, Indians consume enormous quantities of *chicha*, the fermented corn drink of the Incas. And they eat traditional foods: parched corn *tostados*, a boiled corn dish called *mote*, and steaming bowls of the thick vegetable soup *mazamorra*.

Heedless of the hour or the chilling winds, entire families drift from one home to the next, sharing *chicha* and good compay. When they can drink and dance no more, they fall exhausted into sleep as a last inebriated reveller strums a distorted version of the San Juan tune. Miraculously, at dawn they are ready to begin again.

16

CHIMBA LOMA

Yuyaripashün ñaupa tiemlota
Chimba loma tuparishcata
Obscuru vayta jatajüshcagü
Shuti shutimi muyurircangui

Paño sombrero churajüshcagü
Paigüllatan mi muyurimopan
Curi surtijas ñuca cushcagü
Puncha punchami toparimopan

Bosque lomata llucshirimuspa
Silvachihüarca zuleteñita
Puca ruanita churajüshcata
Cushirushpami jüyanï hirca

Remember when long ago
We met again on the mountain opposite.
The dark shawl that you were wearing
Could be seen from far away.

You approached in your felt hat.
It was you who came to me,
On your finger the gold ring that I had given you.
You came that day to find me once again.

In the forest you appeared
And I whistled to you, little Zuleta girl.
I was wearing a red poncho
And joyfully you told me that you loved me.

Quechua song
from the Provinces of Imbabura and Pichincha

From the album *Churay, Churay* by the groups 'Ñanda Mañachi' and
'Bolivia Manta' (Auvidis)

24

26

28

Gold. The fabulous wealth of the Inca Empire. This is what drew the Spanish conquistadores to the Andes in the sixteenth century. But they found little gold in the Ecuadorian Sierra. The Incas destroyed their fabled cities of Quito and Tomebamba, their golden temples of the sun, rather than leave them to the conquering Spaniards.

Nevertheless, the Spanish stayed — to possess the land in the name of their king and the soul of the Indian in the name of their church. They built cities, and hundreds of monasteries and churches decorated with a unique blend of Spanish and Indian art.

The Indians suffered greatly under Spanish colonial rule. Forced labour was not only tolerated, but encouraged. Thus, among the Otavalos of the northern Sierra, who were highly skilled weavers, each community had to fill a quota of men and boys to toil in weaving *obrajes* (workshops). Workers spent at least fourteen hours a day in cold, gloomy buildings which were virtual prisons. An official report from 1666 acknowledges that Indians were beaten and died in chains for offences such as falling asleep on the job or complaining about work conditions.

For three hundred years the Spanish colonial empire exploited the Sierra. Vast properties, called haciendas, were held in feudal ownership and worked by Indians, who were treated like slaves. Independence from Spain in 1822 and the establishment of the Republic of Ecuador in 1830 made little difference in the life of an Indian, for the hacienda economy continued. His father's or grandfather's debt could still keep him bound to the estate.

Until about twenty years ago, many of the Sierra Indians were *huasipungeros*, landless peasants who worked on a hacienda in exchange for a minimum wage and the use of a small field to cultivate for themselves. Some Indians, however, never lost all their lands to the Spanish — the Otavalos, the Salasacas, communities high on the windswept slopes that have held on to their land with unabating passion.

Laws have been written for the Indians' protection; only some have been effective. Nevertheless, little by little, Indians of the Sierra are owning more property. They work to save; to buy fields. They work to still a ceaseless, gnawing hunger to regain their forefathers' land.

Thursday morning. The twin crests of the Illinizas tower in the east; to the west, the white cone of Cotopaxi glows in the first light. Here in the Andes the day begins before dawn. Beneath an infinity of stars, Indians in narrow-brimmed felt hats shoulder massive burdens and leave their small houses. From every direction on the mountain slopes, nimble feet of young and old make their way down precipitous paths. The trails are worn to deep hollows, for generations of families have taken this weekly downward journey to the market in Saquisili.

The market is very old. Before the Spanish came, before the Incas came, Indians from the Amazon basin brought monkeys, parrots and strange herbs to trade in the highlands for salt, blankets and dogs. Curious objects from the jungle on the other side of the Andes still find their way to the Saquisili market — beaks of birds, hoofs of animals, insects with iridescent wings. Even an occasional *tsantsa*, or shrunken head.

A kaleidoscope of swirling colours and forms, the market spreads over eight different plazas, each with its own goods. This is where an Indian comes to find anything he needs from kettles, kerosene lamps and ceramic pots to *shigra* bags and strong rope, both made from plant fibres. He might even look for the right feather to match his pork-pie hat, or for volcanic sulphur, in rock form or yellow powder.

One whole plaza is only for food. There, for a few *sucres*, an Indian can sit at a crowded wooden table and eat his fill of traditional dishes such as *locro* (potato and cheese soup) or roast pork cooked over a charcoal brazier. Not far away, men and women in electric pink and blue ponchos and shawls move among lush piles of tropical harvest from across the mountains. Some of these exotic fruits are split in half to make sure they seem more tempting — lime-green *naranjilla*, coral passion-fruit, velvety white *chirimoya*. Other products come from closer to home: maize, avocados, tomatoes and infinite varieties of that Andean vegetable the Spanish conquistadores first tasted in this area in 1532, the potato.

The liveliest plaza is the animal market — a cacophony of braying donkeys, bellowing cattle and squealing pigs. Few llamas are ever offered for sale; not many remain in Ecuador because the Spanish replaced them as pack animals by donkeys and horses. Almost lost in the din are the high, sharp squeaks of the *cuyes*, the guinea pigs, whose tender meat is considered a great delicacy. They are also a powerful medicine resource. Among Indians such as the Salasacas, a medicine man, or woman, will rub a live guinea pig on the body of a person who is very ill. If the animal does not die within minutes, it means the patient will soon get better. If the animal dies, it is skinned, and under its hide the medicine man finds signs that enable him to diagnose his patient's illness.

By noon, when the sun is directly above Saquisili, most bargains have been closed, most purchases made. The sea of hats begins to ebb away. Slowly, bending under heavy burdens or driving a reluctant ox or pig, families begin the long climb back up the steep, rocky trails. Highways in the Andes circle and curve and take unnecessary time. The Indians prefer to follow the path of the condor, directly over the mountains to home.

The form of Cotopaxi is the most beautiful and the most regular of all that the gigantic peaks of the high Andes present. It is a perfect cone which, clothed in a huge blanket of snow, shines with a dazzling brilliance at sunset and stands out in picturesque fashion against the azure vault of the sky.

Alexander von Humboldt (1824)

I ce on the equator. Nothing in Ecuador is more majestic than its glacial volcanoes. They stand alone — single, monumental peaks well discernible from all the other, lower, Andean peaks which surround them.

More than thirty of these magnificent giants rise from the double row of Andes that line the Sierra's long central valley — the 'Avenue of the Volcanoes', as German scientist Alexander von Humboldt called it. Nearly two centuries later it is still known by that name.

The face of a volcano is as familiar to a Sierra Indian as the face of his own father. It watches over him from the day he is born until the day he dies. The towering presence is an integral part of his daily life. His tiny home nestles at its foot, and his meagre fields are planted in its dry volcanic soil. Its massive form and great snow-crested peak give him a feeling of joy, of security, a point of reference as his bare feet hurry noiselessly over dusty mountain paths.

The names of the volcanoes are ancient and reassuring: Cotopaxi, Cotacachi, Imbabura, Tungurahua, Illiniza, Rumiñahui. The greatest of them all is Chimborazo (6,310 m; 20,702 ft), one of the highest peaks in the entire Andes. Cayambe claims a unique distinction too. Standing right on the equator, its 5,790 m (18,996 ft) summit is the highest point on earth at zero latitude.

Not all are slumbering giants. Though most of Ecuador's thirty-five volcanoes are extinct, eight are still active. Vast destructive forces are hidden within their craters, some of them hundreds of yards wide. Over the ages they accumulate layers of ash and molten lava. And then one day it all erupts. Rising thousands of feet in the air, glowing clouds spill down the mountainside.

The Indians remember (and science has proved) that Cotopaxi erupted on precisely the day the last Inca died more than four centuries ago. But they do not need to look so far back in time for these spectacular displays of a volcano's devastating might.

In 1981, it was Pichincha; in 1974, Reventador. Most active of all is the remote, elusive Sangay; it continuously spits out fumes and ash. But few Indians ever see this smoking colossus, for it is nearly always hidden by dense Amazonian rain-forest clouds.

The volcanoes are an Indian's tangible connection with the eternal. They are older than his people's history. He reveres their wisdom, their power. He ponders their secrets.

May 1735. The proud ship *Portefaix*, of King Louis XV's royal fleet, left La Rochelle sailing west. Among the passengers on board were three French scientists: Charles-Marie de la Condamine, Louis Godin and Pierre Bouguer. They, and a score of assistants, were bound for the ancient realm of Quito; bound for the equator. They could not know then what dramatic events awaited them on the other side of the Atlantic.

What they did know was that the French Academy of Sciences was sending them to solve a question — a question that Europe's scientists had debated avidly for half a century. What is the true geometric shape of the planet?

The only way to solve that question was by measuring a meridian arc — in effect, the circumference of the earth — both at the north pole and at the equator. To accomplish this, the Academy mounted two of the world's earliest scientific expeditions. One went to Lapland; the other was the group which sailed in the *Portefaix* that beautiful morning in May.

La Condamine, who led the equator expedition, described the task facing the scientists in these words: 'It is a matter of making two fixes of latitude, one to the north, the other to the south of the arc, to calculate its amplitude, that is to say what portion it comprises of the circumference of the earth, and its exact measurement in degrees, minutes and seconds. For this it is necessary to make an observation, at each of the two extremities of the arc, of the distance from a star to the zenith. The difference of the two observed distances, or their sum if the star is between the two zeniths, will be the value of the meridian arc.'

The expedition was expected to last several months. But it was 1744 before any of the men returned. Those intervening nine years at the equator were filled with jealousy, intrigue, romance and gross folly; with sickness, danger, violence and death. Only two members of the entire party returned alive to France.

From a scientific perspective, the expedition was successful. It proved definitively Newton's conjecture that the world is not a perfect sphere, that it flattens at the poles and bulges at the equator. As is often the case in scientific investigations, important discoveries were also made which had nothing to do with the main problem being studied. La Condamine sent back to France *Hevea latex*, the key substance from which rubber was later made. And Bouguer's observation that the Andes attracted a plumb line led to the fundamental geophysical concept that mountains, like the tips of icebergs, have deep roots below their visible surface.

A major scientific expedition, such as La Condamine's, did not occur again in the world until exactly one century later. In 1836 the *Beagle* completed its famous voyage. And, once more, the geography of Ecuador helped make scientific history.

The ship stopped for five weeks in the Galápagos Islands — 1,000 km (600 mi.) offshore, yet part of Ecuador. There the *Beagle*'s naturalist, a young Englishman named Charles Darwin, observed that various plants and animals on the Galápagos differed from their ancestral forms on the mainland. Later, this fact became the basis for Darwin's theory of evolution. But even before he left the Galápagos, he wrote: 'Here we seem to be brought somewhat near to that great fact — that mystery of mysteries — the first appearance of new beings on this earth.'

Ingapirca, 'Wall of the Incas' in the Indian's Quechua tongue — the only important Inca ruin that remains in Ecuador. Standing high in the Andes, this small group of buildings with trapezoidal niches and doorways — a hallmark of Inca construction — pays silent tribute to those masters of mortarless stonework.

The history of Ingapirca is lost in Indian memory. It may have been used as a *tambo*, or stopping place, for runners carrying imperial messages from Quito to Tomebamba, the present city of Cuenca, which lies not far away. The main structure, an elliptical platform known as the Temple of the Sun, was probably used for religious rites and other ceremonies.

Cañari Indian schoolchildren swarm up the steps of the Temple, then back down again. They are like a flock of birds in the sky . . . coming together in a cluster . . . spreading apart . . . coming together again. Always moving. A wonderful rhythm against the stillness of the ancient stones.

Later, as the unceasing Andean wind cools their flushed faces, they listen to their teacher tell of the nation that built Ingapirca.

Tahuantinsuyu, the Inca's powerful Empire of the Four Cardinal Points of the World, had its capital at Cuzco. In 1455 it launched an invasion of the Andean kingdoms to the north, the region now known as the Sierra. The fighting was long and bitter. It took twenty years to subdue the kingdoms and make them part of Tahuantinsuyu.

But the vast empire was doomed to extinction. The Inca Ripac foretold its end: pale-faced people — *viracochas*, meaning 'sperm of the ocean' — would come by sea and destroy it. And at that moment, a long-silent volcano would roar its sadness and fury.

In 1526 the Inca conqueror Huayna Cápac died. He left his empire to two sons: Atahualpa ('Great Turkey') was to rule at Quito; Huáscar ('Chain') would rule at Cuzco. This unique division of power did not work, however, and civil war broke out. After six years of fighting, the victor was Atahualpa.

Atahualpa is a name all Sierra Indian children know. His brief life became legend, and history.

The year the civil war ended, 1532, Spanish conquistador Francisco Pizarro arrived in Atahualpa's empire. Saying he had come 'in peace', he asked to meet the Inca ruler. This proved to be a ruse for a treacherous ambush. Atahualpa was taken prisoner and held for a huge ransom — enough gold to fill the room in which he was imprisoned. Treasure poured in from the Inca empire; the ransom was paid. But Atahualpa was not released.

Shamefully going back on his word, Pizarro had the young ruler put on trial, accused of polygamy and incest (both traditional customs among Incas), worshipping false gods, and conspiracy against the King of Spain. The death sentence was inevitable. On the last day of his life, Atahualpa was 'converted' and baptized with Pizarro's first name, in those days the custom with slaves. Then he was strangled like a common criminal.

From deity to slave. From Son of the Sun to non-existence.

With this ignominious chapter, the great Inca empire came to an end on 19 August 1533. Indian rule of the Andes was over, perhaps for all time. And as foretold by Inca prophesy, a long-silent volcano, Cotopaxi, roared its sorrow and rage.

His cape is a cascade of colour, bright as the plumage of tropical birds in the neighbouring Amazon jungle. His stiff black wig hangs low down his back. Bells at his knees mark the rhythm of his dancing. Unique in the Sierra, this costume is seen just once a year, at the Salasaca Indians' largest fiesta — three festivals that merge into one: Corpus Christi, Octava and Chishioctava.

A *banda*, as the multicoloured capes are called, is actually a rod from which strips of damask are hung. Billowing in the brisk Andean wind, it draws all eyes to the *danzante* who wears it. Yet, for the Indians, the *danzantes* are not the major figures at the fiesta. The important men are those who carry bronze-encrusted canes and bear the respected title of *alcalde*.

Without the *alcaldes* there would be no fiesta. These twenty to twenty-five men, who hold their positions for one year, organize — and personally finance — eight out of the twelve annual Salasaca festivals, including the Corpus Christi celebrations. Each *alcalde* hires five entertainers for the year: three *danzantes*, or dancers, and two *maestros*, musicians who play a drum and a *pingullo* flute. This generosity to the community brings the highest honour possible for a Salasaca Indian.

Corpus Christi is a wave of jubilation that floods the Salasaca region. Beginning in late May or early June, the celebrations last nearly a month. Led by the *alcaldes*, hundreds of Indians form dancing processions. Their bare feet shuffling through sienna-coloured earth, they weave through the village and under the rows of arching eucalyptus trees that grow near their small fields.

The spirit of Corpus Christi enters an Indian's blood along with endless amounts of *chicha*. All day long, the *alcaldes'* entertainers wander from house to house providing a fiesta mood. Families gather outside their homes to enjoy the sweet, melancholy notes of a flute and the rhythmic movements of the three *danzantes* resplendent in *bandas* and wigs. Other performers sport boxing gloves, and hide their heads in hairy masks of monkeys or bears. Pink-faced masks, originally meant to mock the white conquistadores, are also worn; one of them is topped by a red 'bishop's mitre' adorned with mirrors and pink plastic dolls. Mirrors — which Indians thought were precious jewels when the Spanish first brought them from Europe — also ornament the *uma tiuctiui*, the heavy red-plume headdress some men wear.

Just before nightfall, the families all gather together in a central place. 'Bears' and 'monkeys' run through the crowd feigning fights, as nearby spectators hurriedly retreat. Hour after hour, the drums keep thumping. Hour after hour, the Indians silently watch the *danzantes'* antics. Their solemn faces and rigid posture give no evidence that they are celebrating their favourite fiesta of the year.

71

An ominous wall of mountain rock — pink, mauve, jade, ochre — rims the Saraguro Indians' horizon. But their history goes far beyond this vivid southern Sierra landscape. Hundreds of years ago, their ancestors lived near Lake Titicaca in Peru, in the heart of the Inca empire.

Early in the fifteenth century, the Inca Yupanqui II began a system of forced colonization known as *mitimaes*. Under this system, entire tribes long under Inca rule were resettled in recently conquered areas of the empire to help establish Inca ways of life in the new territories. As Inca warriors completed the long, difficult conquest of the Ecuadorian Andes, *mitimaes* followed in their wake. The Saraguros came to the southern highlands; the Salasacas, who originally lived in Bolivia, were sent to the central Sierra.

To encourage these tribes to migrate, the Incas offered them gifts of gold and silver bracelets, woollen garments, feathers and coca — so they would work with more zest. The new settlers were also guaranteed certain privileges. They did not have to pay taxes in the first years after their arrival; they were given herds and were provided with enough food to last until their initial harvest. They were also given land, which was divided equally among members of the tribe.

That division still holds for the Salasacas. Land is sold or exchanged, not by square metre, but by *mitmakuna*, the original family plots granted to settlers arriving from Bolivia. The plots are delineated by turquoise hedges of *maguey* plants that border each field.

Inca rule of the Sierra lasted only a few decades, but it changed for ever the lives of the Indians there. Through the *mitimaes* settlers, the Incas introduced their own religion — their reverence for *Inti*, the sun, for the rain, and for *Pachamama*. They imported new foods; they taught advanced agricultural methods, and how to maintain an efficient system of roads. And they established Quechua, with its richly nuanced vocabulary, as the national tongue. It remains the language of the Sierra Indians to this day.

The Quechua spoken by the Saraguros is especially pure, a sign of their particularly close tie with the Incas. These people, who dress all in black except for a white, broad-brimmed hat, say their sombre clothing is a sign of eternal mourning for Atahualpa, the last ruler of the Empire of the Sun.

73

The Indian of the Sierra is, above all, a tiller of the earth. From earliest times, his forefathers worked the land, growing maize, beans, potatoes and small bitter cherries. When the Sun Empire spread into the Sierra, it brought new varieties of root vegetables, such as *yuccas*, *ocas* and sweet potatoes. The new rulers also introduced ways that could greatly increase the earth's yield. The highland farmers learned to use fertilizer, dig irrigation canals and terrace their hillsides, with results that amazed them. Other improvements came with the Spaniards. From them, the Indians learned to cultivate their fields with oxen, horses and iron-tipped tools.

Five o'clock in the morning. Here on the cloud-swept mountain *paramo*, a farmer begins his work in darkness. Before breakfast he sets out from home, driving his oxen before him and balancing a wooden plough on his shoulder. His wife carries a hoe, and a baby on her back. One of the older children brings a bundle of toasted corn for a scanty meal when hunger overtakes them. Throughout the long day, they will all work together: an entire family must share in the continuous struggle for existence at altitudes of 3,000–4,000 m (10,000–13,000 ft).

An immense patchwork of fields stretches up the mountain walls as high as altitude will permit — every bit of it intensively farmed. The type of crops the Indians plant is determined not by seasons but by elevation.

At 2,500 m (8,000 ft), a family will sow mostly maize, beans and peas. As the fields ascend, the ground becomes drier, the nights cooler, and wheat and barley take the place of maize. Still higher, where these European grains cannot survive, native Andean *quinoa*, the 'rice' of the Andes, flourishes. In the highest fields, at altitudes approaching those of the tallest Alpine peaks, the only plant that will grow is a tiny potato, no larger than a chickpea.

The cycle of sowing and reaping follows a rhythm dictated by ancient custom. Days of the week and phases of the moon are important. Farmers sow their seeds on Thursday and Friday, for then 'birds from heaven' do no harm. They plant or harvest at least three days after the new moon, believing that otherwise the crops will rot.

Indians of the Sierra are earthbound people — bound to the timeless pattern of field and seed and harvest; bound to their rooted, stoic temperament. Bound to *Pachamama*. She weaves invisible ties around humans and everything in nature. She nourishes the Indians from birth as she does her *quinoa* and maize. And when they have lived out their days they return to her, buried in her ground like seeds. With profound trust that she cares for their needs, these highland dwellers persevere despite the harsh Andean weather, the stubborn soil and the sombre peaks that form the boundary of their world.

Dusk in the Andes. Scudding patches of fog soften the bleak *paramo* landscape. The venerable white peak of Chimborazo is shrouded in mist. But the Puruhua Indians who live at the foot of the great volcano know that *Taita* Chimborazo ('Father Chimborazo') is there, guarding their mountain existence.

Many Puruhua are shepherds, continuing the work begun by their ancestors back in the sixteenth century, when sheep were first brought to the Andes by the Spanish. Since dawn they have been up on the high mountain meadows. Now they are leading their flocks down a winding trail that threads its way towards home.

Home, the beginning and end of each day's journey to the highland pastures, is a square, windowless, one-room dwelling called a *choza*. On its large porch the Indians do most of their household tasks. The house may be built in the traditional style, of mud and wattle with a pointed roof of *paramo* grass; or it may be made of rammed earth with a tin or Spanish-tile roof. For the Puruhua shepherds, it is the centre of all that life has to give them. The thick walls hold their lives secure, as does the vigilant peak that looms above them.

From around a bend, from behind a slope, the shepherds move forward along the path, wind fluttering their dusty red ponchos like wings. Family after family hurries to reach home with its flocks before the blackness of the equatorial night descends. Now and then someone pauses, calls out a greeting to the sky, a mountain, a bird, a butterfly. For a Sierra Indian, all things in nature are alive; each is personified, referred to as 'she' or 'he'; each has its own spirit, either evil or good.

Guiding their animals down the mountainside, husband and wife work in tandem. As she descends the steep incline, the woman twirls a hand spindle and distaff; spinning, spinning; her hands never idle. Well-trained dogs scamper about, keeping wayward sheep in line. Even the young children help. Trudging barefoot in the cold beside their parents, they brandish small sticks to keep the flock going in the right direction. Children's work is not play in the Andes; it carries true responsibility.

But now the day's work is nearly done. It is dusk, and the families are going home. They are going home to see their 'father'. They are going to see *Taita* Chimborazo.